Smoothies
& Ice Treats

Dedicated to
Smoothie Lovers

Smoothies

& Ice Treats

Lindsay Barnes

&

Amy Shawgo

Back to Basics Products, Inc.
Draper, Utah

Published by:
Back to Basics Products, Inc.
11660 South State Street, Draper, Utah 84020
www.backtobasicsproducts.com

Printed in U.S.A.

ISBN 0-9722418-0-9

Table of Contents

SMOOTHIES

& ICE TREATS

SMOOTHIES. Even the word makes your mouth water. That frozen concoction of fruit and ice that leaves you feeling refreshed and filled. Once the secret domain of fringe health nuts, the smoothie has moved into mainstream and has gone from the juice bar to the kitchen. We have held off as long as we can, wanting to remain undisturbed in our secret garden of healthful bliss. But the public outcry for our healthy, delicious smoothie recipes has grown too great. The wall around our paradise has been thrown done, and we are left with no alternative but to guide the hungry masses of faithful smoothie seekers to a vast new Shangri-La, that they may become one with smoothie bliss.

Fine smoothies are more than a jumble of fruit and ice haphazardly thrown together. Oh sure, you can throw in a little of this and a little of that then keep adding ice until it's thick enough. All smoothies started as experiments. Exceptional smoothies, however, are a carefully crafted blend brought to its peak flavor and consistency through laborious hours of testing, tasting, and testing again. Then comes that moment when the perfect blend is revealed and the ingredients carefully recorded.

We hope you have as much fun with the recipes in this book as we had coming up with them. So get some ice and fruit and lets start making smoothies!

INTRODUCTION

YOU ARE WHAT YOU EAT! What you eat affects your appearance, your health and the way you feel. Ultimately you control your nutritional state by what and how much you eat, but with the help of the Smoothie Elite we can make it fun, easy and delicious. Smoothies have always been an easy way to get the nutrients and vitamins we need to make our bodies healthy. We can have them on the go for a delicious quick breakfast, an energy enhancement lunch or a healthy mid-afternoon snack. It is definitely a simple, tasty way to get a nutrient packed meal! The great thing about smoothies is that everybody can make them and everybody loves them. Our smoothie recipes come in many varieties for different tastes, likes and types. There are great smoothies that contain ingredients specifically for the health of men, women, children, athletes and the health conscious to name a few. There are also wonderful smoothies to improve your health, maintain and repair your body, relieve and relax or just to satisfy your taste buds! So let loose and have fun with our healthy recipes and tips or try experimenting with some of your own. Our simple to use Smoothie Elite, recipe book and nutritional tips are a great start to improving your overall health and quality of life with delicious, appetizing smoothies.

TIPS TO A HEALTHY DIET

The characteristics of an excellent diet should include a combination of 5 things:
- Variety
- Moderation
- Adequacy
- Balance
- Calorie Control

These 5 keys to a healthy balanced diet are all incorporated and implemented into our booklet and recipes.

So how do we know what is good for our bodies? First we must have a basic knowledge of nutrition and healthy eating. So, to start we must learn about the fundamental concepts to building the body through nutrition, which includes Proteins, Carbohydrates, and Fats.

CARBOHYDRATES

Ultimately carbohydrates provide fuel to run the body. Carbohydrates come in 2 forms: complex carbohydrates (starches) and simple carbohydrates (sugars). Sugar provides a quick boost whereas starches have a more lasting effect and contain many vitamins, minerals, and other important nutrients for the body. The main source of carbohydrates should come from starches or complex carbohydrates, since they are more dense in nutrients. Some of the best forms of carbohydrates include: fruits, grains, legumes, starches, and vegetables. Foods high in simple carbohydrates should be avoided. These include foods such as cakes, candy, and cookies, which are very high in sugars and fats yet low in vitamins and minerals. Complex carbohydrates can also be a key in weight management. The digestive system uses up more energy in metabolizing starches than it does in fat. These complex carbohydrates are also good at recognizing when enough food has been consumed and therefore signals our bodies when we are full.

PROTEINS

Proteins are known as "building blocks" for muscles, bones, teeth, hair, and fingernails. Proteins build and rebuild tissues in the body and regulate chemical functions. Protein structure is a part of every cell. It aids in growth and maintenance and helps in the resistance of infections. The best proteins to intake are what is known as 'complete proteins' which contains all essential amino acids. Complete proteins include:

- Dairy Products – milk, yogurt, cheese
- Eggs
- Grains – wheat germ
- Nuts – walnuts, black
- Soy Products
- Vegetables – collards, spinach

It's possible to combine incomplete proteins for the desired effect of a complete protein. Incomplete proteins include some of the items listed below:

- Legumes – peanuts, beans, peas
- Wheat – white flour, wild rice, rye, cornmeal
- Nuts – almonds, cashews, pecans
- Vegetables – asparagus, corn, mushrooms, potatoes

FATS

Fats in minimal use are important in performing bodily functions. Fats aid in storing energy, maintaining healthy hair and skin, providing essential fatty acids, and alerting the body when it is full and satisfied. Fats are also important in providing and carrying fat-soluble vitamins A, D, E, and K. But of course too much or the wrong kind of fat can be destructive to the body. Good fats include those that come naturally from foods, which include; cold water fish (salmon, trout, tuna), sunflower/olive/sesame oil, avocados, and raw nuts. Fats that are bad include those that have been processed and are usually high glycemic carbohydrates. These carbohydrates cause the body to secrete higher levels of the fat storage hormone, insulin. The over consumption of fat is one of the principal nutrition-related problems for Americans. Is it surprising that the three leading causes of death (heart disease, cancer and stroke) are all diet related?

DAILY RECOMMENDATIONS

The United States Department of Agriculture created what Americans know as the Food Guide Pyramid. This was created in order to give people a basic knowledge or guide of what

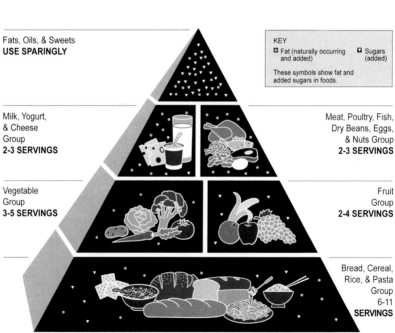

Food Guide Pyramid
A Guide to Daily Food Choices

Fats, Oils, & Sweets
USE SPARINGLY

KEY
▢ Fat (naturally occurring and added) ▣ Sugars (added)
These symbols show fat and added sugars in foods.

Milk, Yogurt, & Cheese Group
2-3 SERVINGS

Meat, Poultry, Fish, Dry Beans, Eggs, & Nuts Group
2-3 SERVINGS

Vegetable Group
3-5 SERVINGS

Fruit Group
2-4 SERVINGS

Bread, Cereal, Rice, & Pasta Group
6-11
SERVINGS

Source: U.S. Department of Agriculture/U.S. Department of Health and Human Services

our body needs daily. The pyramid is a visual guide that specifies the minimum number of daily servings for each of the food groups. It puts an emphasis on the 5 groups in the lower part of the Pyramid. It is important to note that each food group provides some of the nutrients needed for healthy living, but not all. That is why it is important to have a combination of foods. One group cannot replace another, nor is one group more important than another. For the best quality of life you need them all. It is important to remember the best diet is a low-fat, high-fiber diet rich in potassium, low in sodium and that contains antioxidants (fruits and vegetables), which are also important in reducing the risk of heart disease and stroke. Think of it... medicine that tastes good!

SERVING SIZE

DAIRY
- 1 cup (8oz.) milk or yogurt
- 2 slices of cheese (1fi oz.)
- 2 cups cottage cheese

MEAT
- 2–3 oz cooked lean meat, poultry, fish
- 1 large egg
- ½–1 cup cooked beans

VEGETABLES
- ½ cup vegetable
- ¾ cup vegetable juice
- 1 cup raw leafy vegetables

FRUIT
- 1 piece fruit/melon wedge
- ¾ cup fruit juice
- ½ cup canned fruit

GRAINS

- 1 slice bread
- ½ cup cooked rice, pasta or cereal
- 1 cup cold cereal

FOOD GROUP BENEFITS

Each food group contributes to your overall health in its own way. Listed below you will find each grouping of food and what types of basic nutrients they give you and what in turn these do for your body.

FRUITS

Fruits give us:

- Vitamin A
- Vitamin C
- Potassium
- Folic Acid
- Fiber

The benefits are:

- Helps skin and aids in vision (Vitamin A).
- Heals and fights infections (Vitamin C)
- Maintains heart beat, regulates fluid, and aids in muscle/functions (Potassium)
- Helps growth, cell division, and blood cells (Folic Acid)
- Aids digestion of food   (Fiber)

VEGETABLES

Vegetables give us:

- Vitamin A
- Vitamin C
- Folic Acid
- Fiber
- Magnesium
- Iron

The benefits are:
- Necessary for muscle/nerve functioning
- Found in bones (magnesium)
- Carries oxygen in red blood cells/muscles (Iron)
- Helps skin and aids in vision (Vitamin A)
- Heals and fights infections (Vitamin C)
- Helps growth, cell division and blood cells (Folic Acid)
- Aids digestion of food (Fiber)

MEATS
Meats give us:
- Protein
- Vitamin B
- Iron
- Zinc

The benefits are:
- Aids in growth, replacement, & maintenance of body tissues (Protein)
- Helps in use of energy in the body (Vitamin B)
- Carries oxygen in red blood cells/muscles (Iron)
- Heals, gives taste perception, growth and sexual development (Zinc)

DAIRY
Dairy gives us:
- Calcium
- Riboflavin
- Protein

The benefits are:
- Aids in development and maintenance of bones and teeth (Calcium)
- Helps the body use energy (Riboflavin)

• Aids in growth, replacement, & maintenance of body tissues (Protein)

GRAINS

Grains give us:
- Carbohydrates
- Fiber
- Vitamin B
- Iron

The benefits:
- Body's major source of energy (Carbohydrates)
- Aids digestion of food (Fiber)
- Helps in use of energy in the body (Vitamin B)
- Carries oxygen in red blood cells/muscles (Iron)

TIPS TO HEALTH & QUALITY OF LIFE

It is important to keep in mind that in order to reach optimal physical health we must include exercise in our nutritional habits. The physiological benefits of exercises include decreased blood pressure, elevated metabolism so more calories are burned, improved muscle tone, increased breakdown and use of fat, increased HDL (good) cholesterol, strengthened heart, decreased chance of osteoporosis, increased efficiency of the digestive system, and controlled weight. It is suggested when exercising we emphasize frequency, intensity, time, and the type of exercise we do. The general guidelines for exercise include:
- Frequency: 3-5 days a week
- Intensity: exercise within your personal "target range"
- Time: 20-30 minutes of continuous exercise
- Type: Aerobic exercise (continually for 20-30 min.) combined with anaerobic exercise

These exercise tips combined with controlling what you eat can improve your overall health and the type of life you live both physically and mentally. It is pertinent to our longevity and quality of life to get the recommended physical exercise and nutrition intake appropriate for our bodies.

HOW DOES THIS KNOWLEDGE HELP US?

Now that you know a basic knowledge of what is important to include and not include in your diet and exercise regiment, this will help you to make intelligent, knowledgeable decisions about your lifestyle. You will be able to use the recipes contained in this book to better your eating habits and become aware of your nutritional intake. This also allows you to adjust and create your own nutritional blend to what is personally needed for your body. The recipes included have taken into consideration variety, moderation, balance, calorie control, adequacy, and of course flavor as they were created. And with all of the different recipes offered, it is possible to drink healthy, nutrient-dense smoothies to help you reach your optimal nutritional health goals.

TIPS TO MAKING A GREAT SMOOTHIE

EXPERIMENT

Let your taste buds be your guide. Only you know what you like best, so be a little creative and add your own ingredients or take some ingredients away. Don't be afraid to try something different and new!

CONSISTENCY

The consistency of course will depend greatly on the blender you use. Be sure to use a blender that thoroughly smooths out all those chunks of ice or frozen fruit. Things to look for are a good ice-crushing blade and a strong, efficient motor. We used the Back to Basics Smoothie Pro™ to test our recipes for this book. The easy dispensing valve and stir stick helped us create a lot of smoothies in a short time.

If a smoothie is too thick or too thin add either more of the suggested liquids to make thinner or more of the suggested frozen ingredients (fruit, yogurt, ice, sherbet, ice-cream etc.) to make thicker.

TEXTURE
If you like really smooth smoothies be sure to use crushed ice instead of ice cubes. And if seeds bother you in your smoothie, you may want to get out the strainer.

TASTE
If your smoothie is a little to tart or sweet, calm it down with milk, plain yogurt, and/or ice. If your smoothie isn't quite sweet enough, add juice, a touch of sugar, honey, or syrup.

SUBSTITUTE
Again, be creative! If the recipe calls for apple juice and you don't have it, try a different type of juice or even milk. If you don't have fresh fruit, canned fruit also tastes great in smoothies. If you are missing an ingredient, use what you have at home or don't use it at all.

TIMING
After making your smoothies, serve immediately. Smoothies are definitely best when served soon after they are made! If they sit too long they may get a little runny or inconsistent.

HEALTH

For the healthiest smoothies, we suggest using low-fat or non-fat products and fresh fruit. Any of the ingredients in our recipes can be substituted with low-fat or non-fat substitutions and still taste great. It will help to keep calorie and fat intake to a minimum, without missing out on a tasty treat.

SMOOTHIES TO

MAINTAIN &
REPAIR THE BODY

ONE OF THE BEST DEFENSES against infection and disease is getting the proper amount of fruits and vegetables in your diet. These nutrient-dense foods contribute to maintaining and repairing many parts of our bodies and without them it would be very difficult to live a long, healthy life. They provide our bodies with the necessary vitamins and nutrients for muscle and nerve functions, healing and fighting infections, maintaining regular heart beat, regulating fluids in the body, aiding in the digestion of food, and maintaining healthy skin and vision. So, let's mix up and drink up some great tasting smoothies below to help our bodies stay young and feeling great!

*Note: To make smoothies thinner add extra amounts of the suggested liquids. To make thicker, add ice.

MANGO TANGO

Get up and do the tango, because with this smoothie you will live long and healthy with the nutrients packed in this blend. Mangoes are a terrific source of potassium, beta-carotene, and insoluble fiber, which aid in low blood pressure, strong immune systems and a healthy hearts.

　　¾ cup pineapple juice or orange juice
　　1 sliced banana
　　1 cup pineapple sherbet
　　2 cups mango slices
　　2 cups ice

PEACH REFRESHER

What could be more refreshing than drinking to your health? Peaches give us the sources that help our bodies prevent infections, cancers, heart diseases, and strokes. They also contain nutrients that decrease blood pressure and menopausal symptoms. So, here's drinking to your health!

　　¾ cup peach nectar or apple juice
　　1 sliced banana
　　1 cup low-fat peach yogurt
　　2 cups peach slices
　　2 cups ice

BLUEBERRY BLAST

Similar to the cranberry, the blueberry contains the same agents know to soothe and prevent bladder infections. This powerful blast of blueberry will soothe, relieve, and taste great.

2 cups blueberries

1 cup raspberries

½ cup cran-raspberry juice or milk

1 cup low-fat blueberry yogurt

2 cups ice

VITAMIN C ATTACK

One of the best things to do for the flu is to drink a lot of liquids that are dense with vitamin C. Let's do as the doctor ordered and get some rest and drink the Vitamin C Attack.

2–3 cups sliced watermelon

1 cup sliced cantaloupe

¼ cup strawberries

1 cup low-fat plain yogurt

2–3 cups ice

VEGGIE DELIGHT

This sweet tasting, veggie based smoothie is a great way to add some variety to your diet and some health to your life! Apples are great for regulating blood sugar, cholesterol, and colon function. You'll also be delighted to know that carrots are a great source of vitamin C and folate.

1 cup apple juice
1 cup sliced red apple
½ cup applesauce
½ cup sliced carrots
½ cup cucumber peeled and sliced
2 ½ cups ice

PAPAYA PLEASURE

Papaya has a great source of papain, which is known to aid in the digestive function. This sweet tasting, smooth textured treat will glide down smoothly and keep you feeling healthy.

2 cups sliced papaya
½ cup pineapple chunks
½ sliced banana
1 cup pineapple sherbet
¾ cup low-fat milk
2 cups ice

FEELING 'GRAPE'?

This grape tasting smoothie has a fresh crisp taste that also contains an important nutrient known as resveratrol. Resveratrol is known to hinder the development of cancer. The 'Feeling Grape' smoothie will leave you feeling great!

2 cups red seedless grapes

½ cup grape juice

1 cup lime sherbet

2 cups ice

PINEAPPLE PLEASURE

We all know sore throats can be miserable, but did you know that pineapples can act as an anti-inflammatory to soothe those awful sore throats? Well, it's true! So when you feel your throat start to tighten up, remember the 'Pineapple Pleasure'.

1½ cup frozen pineapple chunks

½ cup frozen raspberries

1 cup pineapple sherbet

½ cup raspberry juice or low-fat milk

1 peeled and sliced kiwi

2 cups ice

ALL ABOUT APRICOTS

Apricots are a great source of beta-carotene, which is transformed into vitamin A by our bodies. Vitamin A is essential for proper vision, growth and reproduction.

2 cups sliced apricot

1 cup apricot nectar

1½ cup low-fat vanilla ice cream

2½ cups ice

APPLE A DAY

We've all he heard that an apple a day keeps the doctor away, but is it true? Well, it can surely help! Apples have a deliciously sweet taste that isn't to overpowering and they also contain pectin, which helps regulate cholesterol.

1 cup low-fat plain yogurt

1 cup slice green apple with skin

½ tsp. ground cinnamon

1 cup lime sherbet

1 cup apple juice

2 cups ice

PROTEIN SHAKE

This quick and healthy treat is loaded with protien and essential vitamins and minerals. It's a great supplement if you are working out and need to grow lean muscle.

¼ cup chocolate-flavored whey protein powder

¼ cup chocolate-flavored Slimfast™ powder

1 banana

1 cup skim milk

1 cup ice

SMOOTHIES

F O R
ATHLETES

ATHLETES NEED to understand the importance of a
healthy diet. During vigorous exercise our bodies are depleted
of many important nutrients and vitamins used to function, so
it is essential that we restore and replenish what we have used.
It is also necessary for our bodies to get the needed nutrients
before a workout for optimal performance and to decrease the
chances of injury. Any serious athlete will tell you what a dif-
ference a nutritional diet can do for your workout-wonders! So
get ready to enhance your performance with the next variety of
smoothies. This section contains some great suggestions for a
wonderful variety of smoothies for athletes. Some of the
smoothies below aid in building muscle, some are packed with
carbs for a blast of energy, and some contain agents that
relieve your aches and pains after a tough work out! And
you'll never believe it, they all taste great!

CHERRY REPAIRIE

Cherries are great for those of you who watch your weight by exercising. Cherries contain vitamin C and anthocyanin, which helps to maintain and repair connective tissue. This is great news for the athlete since exercise puts constant stress on those tissues.

2 cups pitted cherries
¾ cup raspberry juice
1 cup low-fat vanilla or cherry yogurt
¾ cup raspberry sherbet
2 cups ice

ISLAND FRUIT BLAST

Many times during exercise our body is depleted of many important vitamins and minerals that must be replenished. This nutrient dense smoothie will help do just that!

1 cup pineapple juice
1 cup non-fat raspberry sherbet
1 cup slice mango
½ cup frozen raspberries
1 sliced banana
2 cups ice

PROTEIN POWER

For those of you who want to build a little muscle while working out, it is pertinent to get protein in your diet. It's great for building muscles and repairing body tissue.

1½–2 cups milk

2 tablespoons dry chocolate milk mix

½ teaspoon dry chocolate pudding mix

¼ cup peanut butter

1 sliced banana

2 cups ice

GUAVA PACKED SNACK

Vitamin C can help safeguard our bodies from exercise induced injuries as it protects the muscles we use in exercise related activities.

1 cup guava nectar

1 cup sliced peaches

1 cup slice mango

1 cup raspberry sherbet

2 cups ice

PINEAPPLE PEACH PLEASER

Pineapple acts as and anti-inflammatory and helps to soothe those sore, inflamed muscles. So after a tough workout, come home and relax those muscles with the Pineapple Peach Pleaser.

$\frac{3}{4}$ cup pineapple juice

2 cups pineapple chunks

$\frac{1}{2}$ cup peaches

1 sliced banana

1 cup pineapple sherbet

2 cups ice

RASPBERRY RELIEVER

This creamy tasting raspberry smoothie will help to minimize those after workout aches and pains. Raspberries contain a type of natural aspirin source that will definitely be a relief to your body.

$\frac{3}{4}$ cup low fat milk

2 cups raspberries

1 cup low-fat raspberry sherbet or yogurt

$\frac{1}{2}$ banana

2 cups ice

CARBO CREATION

Many athletes know that getting plenty of carbs before work-ing out will give you the energy to last and endure throughout your exercise regiment or competition. This carbo packed smoothie will help you achieve your exercise goals!

1 cup apple juice
1 cup slice peaches
¼ cup blueberries
½ cup strawberries
1 cup vanilla yogurt
2½ cups ice

SMOOTHIES FOR

STRESS
MANAGEMENT

FOR THE STRESSES IN YOUR LIFE, how about a smoothie? Did you know that if the nutritional status of a person is poor, they are unable to respond properly and effectively to stressful situations? This in turn causes more stress and makes a person more susceptible to infections. Stress is also associated with health issues including cancer and heart disease. All the busy things we spend doing in our day triggers stress not only physically, but also mentally and emotionally. So, lets bring out the vitamins and nutrients that are essential in reducing stress and preventing infections caused by stress!

　　*Note: To make smoothies thinner add extra amounts of the suggested liquids. To make thicker add ice.

SMOOTHIE SOOTHING INSOMNIA

The lack of calcium may cause some symptoms of nerve sensitivity, irritability and/or insomnia. That is why this calming smoothie was specifically packed full of calcium and potassium. The potassium in cantaloupe aids in the stress response and the ingredient honey acts as a sleeping tool that adds sweetness to the drink. So jump in bed with the smoothie soothing insomnia blend, because tonight you'll be getting a good nights sleep.

$\frac{1}{2}$ cup soymilk or milk

1 cup plain yogurt

1 cup chopped cantaloupe

1 cup chopped watermelon

1 sliced banana

1 tbs. of honey

2 cups ice

CRAN-RASPBERRY RELAXER

After a hard days work, what could sound more refreshing than a raspberry relaxer. The magnesium in raspberries and blueberries can act like a sedative and help to relax the muscles in the body. Start up the smoothie maker and relax.

$\frac{1}{2}$ cup cran-raspberry juice

2 cups raspberries

$\frac{1}{2}$ cup blueberries

1 cup raspberry sherbet

2 cup ice

*add $\frac{1}{2}$ cup carrot juice for extra magnesium

BANANA BREAK

Bananas are a great source of potassium which aids the body during the stress response. So take a break from your stressful day and drink something that is deliciously creamy and tasty.

1 sliced banana

1 cup limeade

1 cup lime sherbet

$\frac{1}{2}$ cup non-fat banana yogurt

2 cups ice

STRESS-FREE STRAWBERRY

Many times during stressful periods in our lives our bodies quickly use up our supply of vitamins and nutrients that we use for daily activities. We must remember that it is important to replenish what has been used. This drink is packed with many of those nutrients and vitamins that need to be restocked!

2 cups strawberries

½ cup strawberry nectar or low-fat milk

1 cup peaches

1 cup low-fat plain yogurt

2 cups ice

LEMON TO YOUR AIDE

Yogurt contains a natural sleeping aid called tryptophan. Tryptophan is an amino acid that is known to induce sleep. This delicious smoothie has a light and creamy taste with a touch of lemon.

¾ cup lemonade

1½ cup raspberries or strawberries

1 cup low-fat lemon yogurt

1 sliced banana

2 cups ice

SMOOTHIE BALANCER

Simply having a healthy balanced diet can help the body to maintain balance and structure, which in turn helps the body to be ready for any stressful situation. Here is a smoothie that is a great start for balancing your diet and reducing stress.

1 cup orange juice

1 cup strawberries (or fruit of your choice)

¼ cup bran cereal

½ cup low-fat strawberry yogurt (or yogurt of your choice)

¼ cup chopped carrots

2 cups ice

IT'S LIME TIME

Zinc is very helpful mineral during times of stress. It is aids in replenishing the hormones we use during stressful situations. Yogurt is a great way to get the zinc you need and also a great way to help make your smoothie perfectly smooth!

1 cup low-fat milk
1 cup low-fat lime sherbet
½ cup lime slices
½ cup raspberries
2 cups ice

LEMONADE WATERMELON SOOTHER

2 cups watermelon pulp

3 oz frozen lemonade concentrate ($\frac{1}{2}$ of a 6 oz. can)

1 cup lemon/lime soda

1 tsp. grenadine syrup

1–2 cups ice, to desired consistency

*may need to add water

PEPPERMINT FLOAT

2 cups low-fat frozen vanilla yogurt

2 cups milk

2 tbs. crushed peppermint candy

1$\frac{1}{2}$ cups ice

SMOOTHIES FOR

THE HEALTH CONSCIOUS

NUTRITIONAL BLENDS are a great way to cut down on your calorie and fat intake. Fresh fruit and vegetable smoothies can be flavorful and filling without the unnecessary fats and preservatives that often lead to weight gain. It's been proven that foods high in carbohydrates are often times low in calories, making them great for your body. These fiber-rich foods, high in carbs are other wise known as fruits and vegetables. So as long as the calories you intake, don't exceed that which you expend, it makes it much easier for you to lose or maintain a healthy weight. Carbs are also a terrific energy source, keeping you moving and on your toes all day. So, when your on the go, or not, replace a meal with a satisfying smoothie and get a great variety of needed nutrients and vitamins.

*Note: To make smoothies thinner add extra amounts of the suggested liquids. To make thicker, add ice.

IN 'GRAPE' SHAPE

While trying to lose weight, it is important to get a good source of potassium in your diet. Grapes are a great way to restore your body with this much-needed nutrient.

2 cups red seedless grapes
½ cup sparkling grape juice
½ cup boysenberries
½ cup blueberries
2 cup ice

GOING GRAPEFRUITIE

This smoothie is definitely low in calories and tart to the taste. It is a great blend that also aids in the reduction of cholesterol.

1½ cup fresh squeezed grapefruit juice
1 banana
1½ cup low-fat vanilla yogurt
2½ cups ice

MELON BERRY SPLASH

Melons are a great low-calorie fruit, rich in flavor and potassium. Potassium is used when the body expends energy or simply exercises. Fruits are an important, necessary way in which we replenish that supply of potassium. This great low cal treat is perfect for those who exercise and eat right in order to achieve that much desired waistline.

1 cup sliced cantaloupe
1 cup sliced honeydew
¼ cup strawberries
½ cup non-fat/skim milk
¾ cup low-fat strawberry yogurt
2 cups ice

CHOCOLATE LOVERS LOW-FAT SMOOTHIE

For those of you who can't resist the sweet taste of chocolate, but feel guilty every time you give in, try this low-fat, great-tasting chocolate surprise. Not only will you love it, but you will feel good about loving it. Indulge, partake, and feel great!

2 tbs. dry chocolate mix

½ tsp. dry low fat pudding mix

1½ cup non-fat/skim milk

½ tsp. vanilla extract

2 cups ice

½ cup raspberries (optional)

KIWI-BERRY SENSATION

Kiwi contains many essential vitamins necessary for good health. It has also been thought that some of these vitamins, particularly A and E, work against the effects of fat on the body.

2 sliced kiwis
2 cups strawberries
½ cup kiwi-strawberry juice
1 cup low-fat plain yogurt
2 cups ice

APRICOT & BLACKBERRY BLEND

Both of these delicious fruits are low fat and great at keeping you regular, while you are watching your weight.

1½ cups sliced apricots
1 cup sliced nectarines
½ cup apricot nectar
¼ cup frozen blackberries
2 cups ice

WATERMELON WAISTLINE

This sweet tasting, light-filling smoothie is great for the health conscious. And although watermelon is a fruit bursting with flavor, it is very low in sugar and calories and is a great antioxidant.

2½ cups chopped watermelon
1 cup low-fat raspberry sherbet
2 cups ice

CRANBERRY SPRITZER

With only 145 calories, and 1 gram of fat per serving, this health conscious smoothie is a delicious way to satisfy your sweet tooth!

2 cups cranberry juice
½ cup club soda
½ cup low fat vanilla yogurt
1 cup ice
Garnish with mint sprigs if desired.

LOW-FAT STRAWBERRY ORANGE

2 cups strawberries
½ cup orange juice
1 cup skim milk
1 cup plain nonfat yogurt
1 cup ice

SUPER HEALTHY SHAKE

1 cup non-fat vanilla yogurt
1 banana
1 cup frozen strawberries or peaches
4 oz. frozen orange juice concentrate

SMOOTHIES

FOR
WOMEN

WOMEN HAVE THEIR OWN nutritional needs that must be addressed continuously for optimal health. Many times we are so busy with the many different roles we play that our nutritional goals are set aside. However, it is absolutely essential to keep in mind our mental and physical health in order to live happy, healthy lives. Following are sensible smoothies for the women of today. Each blend contains essential nutrients and vitamins to keep you on your toes and ready for any task.

   *Note: To make smoothies thinner add extra amounts of the suggested liquids. To make thicker, add ice.

BERRY BONE BOOSTER

The bone booster is a calcium packed, flavorful treat, which will help any women in the prevention of osteoporosis. Calcium aids in developing and maintaining bones and teeth, making you strong and in control. Combined with the sweet fresh taste of a wonderful combination of berries, this will be an unforgettable healthy treat!

$\frac{1}{2}$ cup strawberries

$\frac{1}{2}$ cup raspberries

$\frac{1}{2}$ cup boysenberries

1 cup low-fat plain or raspberry yogurt

$\frac{1}{2}$ cup low fat or fat free milk

2 cups ice

SOOTHING PEACH

This creamy smoothie is rich in ingredients that help soothe menstrual aches and pains. Calcium and soy protein are known to help prevent mood alterations and reduce cramps and headaches. The vitamin C in peaches aids in fighting against infections and reducing the risk of heart disease, strokes and cancer. Medicine that tastes great!

$\frac{1}{4}$ cup low fat/fat free milk

$\frac{1}{4}$ cup soymilk

1 cup low fat/nonfat peach yogurt

2 cups sliced peaches

2 cups ice

CRANBERRY COOLER

Cranberries are not only soothing, they also help prevent bladder infections. Here is a cool cranberry drink that will help your body fight against this infection. Its cool, crisp taste will soothe and relieve.

1 cup cranberries
1 cup raspberries
½ cup cran-raspberry juice
1 cup raspberry yogurt
2 cups ice

CRISP CARROT CONCOCTION

This delicious veggie drink is a perfect match for every woman. Not only does it have a great variety of nutrients and vitamins, but a great variety of taste. Carrots are terrific for easing menopausal symptoms and they also aid in preventing breast cancer.

1 cup sliced carrots
½ cup apple juice
½ cup applesauce
¼ cup sliced celery
½ cup low fat milk
2 cups ice

BOUNTIFUL BLACKBERRIES

Blackberries are great for women and decreasing their chances of heart disease. So here's to a strong, healthy heart!

2 cups blackberries

½ cup blueberries

1 cup low-fat blueberry yogurt

½ cup low-fat/nonfat milk

2 cups ice

ESPECIALLY FOR EXPECTING MOTHERS

This fruit packed smoothie is a great combination of sweet, juicy flavors. Not only is it a terrific blend, but the oranges are terrific for expecting mothers. Oranges contain folic acid, which is known to protect against birth defects.

½ cup milk

½ cup orange juice

½ cup vanilla yogurt

½ cup slice mango

1 sliced banana

1 tbs. orange juice concentrate

½ tsp. vanilla

2 cups ice

SMOOTHIES

F O R

M E N

MEN HAVE THEIR OWN nutritional needs that must be addressed for optimal health. Many times we are so busy with the many different roles we play that our nutritional goals are set aside. However, it is absolutely essential to keep in mind our mental and physical health in order to live happy, healthy lives. Following are sensible smoothies for the men of today. Each blend contains essential nutrients and vitamins to keep you on your toes and ready for any task.

TASTY TOMATO SMOOTHIE

This tasty tomato smoothie is a creamy, smooth, nutrient packed drink that is great for men's health. Nutrients in the tomato act as antioxidants, and these same chemicals aid in preventing prostate cancer.

2 cups of chopped tomatoes
½ cup tomato juice
½ cup apple juice
½ cup sliced carrots
½ cup chopped celery
1 tsp. minced onion
Tabasco™ sauce (to taste)
2 cups ice (optional)

PEAR BERRY PERFECTION

Pears are wonderful for preventing strokes and high blood pressure. Sipping on this smoothie will give men the long lasting health they desire.

3 cups sliced pears
1 cup strawberry nectar
¼ cup strawberries
2 cups ice

TOTALLY TART

The Totally Tart smoothie has a different, but delicious taste, that will keep your sweet tooth satisfied and your heart at ease. Grapefruit is great fruit for those with heart disease because they contain agents that lower blood pressure, lower cholesterol and help arteries.

1½ cup fresh squeezed grapefruit juice
¼ cup pineapple juice
½ cup sliced pineapple
1 cup low-fat plain yogurt
½ cup low-fat frozen vanilla ice cream
2 cups ice

COCONUT DREAM

Men who are thinking about fatherhood also need to make sure they are getting a variety of appropriate nutrients in their diets. Also, Vitamin E can help to make conception more possible!

½ cups low fat milk
⅓ cup grated coconut
2 cups sliced strawberries
¼ tbs. honey
2 cups ice

SMOOTHIES

F O R
K I D S

KIDS LOVE SMOOTHIES! They like to make them, and they love to drink them. The smoothie is a great way to make sure your kids get enough calcium, vitamins, and the recommended servings of fruits and vegetables. They're good – good for you, and just plain fun!

RASPBERRY CREAM

1 cup low fat vanilla or raspberry yogurt
¼ cup milk
1 cup frozen raspberries
¾ cup frozen strawberries
2 cups ice

CHOCOLATE TREAT

3.5 oz. package of instant chocolate pudding mix
1½ cups milk
1½ cups ice
1 banana

BERRY VITAMIN PACKED

$\frac{1}{2}$ cup strawberries

$\frac{1}{2}$ cup blueberries

$\frac{1}{2}$ cup blackberries

$\frac{1}{2}$ cup chopped carrot

1 cup milk

1 cup apple juice

2 cups ice

BANANA SPLIT SMOOTHIE

Your kids will love this smooth and creamy beverage that tastes just like a banana split. They'll never know its good for them too.

2 bananas

1 can (8 oz) crushed pineapple, drained

$1\frac{1}{2}$ cups milk

$\frac{1}{2}$ cup sliced strawberries (fresh or frozen)

2 tbs. honey

1 cup ice

PURPLE COW

2 cups vanilla ice cream
6 tbs. frozen grape juice concentrate
1 cup milk
1 cup ice

PEACH PLEASER

2 cups canned peaches
1 cup milk
2 cups vanilla ice cream
½ tsp. almond extract
1 can (6 oz) frozen orange juice concentrate

CHOCOLATE MUDSLIDE

1 cup skim milk

1 banana

2 tbs. honey

¼ cup chocolate milk drink mix, or hot cocoa drink mix

½ cup low-fat vanilla yogurt

BERRY BANANA FRUIT SMOOTHIE

1 banana

1 cup raspberry or strawberry yogurt

¾ cup unsweetened pineapple juice

½ cup ice

ORANGE APRICOT TASTE TWISTER

2 cups orange sherbet
1 can chilled apricot nectar
1 tbs. frozen orange juice concentrate
1½ cups milk
1 cup ice
*garnish with orange zest if desired

RASPBERRY CHOCOLATE CREAMIE

1 cup frozen raspberries
1 banana
2 tbs. instant chocolate pudding powder
1 cup cream soda
1 cup milk
2 cups ice

PINEAPPLE BANANA SLUSH

1 tbs. frozen orange juice concentrate
1 tbs. frozen lemonade concentrate
1 banana
2 tbs. sugar
1 cup pineapple juice
1 cup lemon lime soda
1 cup ice

MAKE IT A MEAL
BREAKFAST
SMOOTHIES

WHETHER YOU'RE IN A HURRY, dieting, or just tired of the same old fare. Making you meal a smoothie has health, taste, and time benefits!

What better way to start your day than with a refreshing blend of fruits, veggies, and other nutritious foods. It's a proven fact that if you begin your day with a healthy breakfast you are better able to concentrate, have more energy, and get more accomplished in the morning. These smoothies will give you the energy you need to make your day a success.

STRAWBERRY YOGURT SHAKE

We know we should include each of the four food groups in our morning meal. In today's fast paced world who has time for whole wheat toast, fruit, and a glass of milk. Why not throw it all in the smoothie maker, and you've got a quick healthy breakfast that tastes great.

2 cups low fat, plain yogurt
1 cup milk
$\frac{1}{2}$ cup honey
$1\frac{1}{2}$ cups frozen strawberries
$\frac{1}{4}$ cup toasted wheat germ
$\frac{1}{4}$ tsp. almond extract
dash salt

BERRY VITAMIN PACKED BREAKFAST

This delicious smoothie is packed with vitamins to help get you off to a great start in the morning. It's great for kids in a rush to get to school. They'll love the taste and won't even notice the hidden vegetables. Use frozen berries for added convenience!

$\frac{1}{2}$ cup strawberries
$\frac{1}{2}$ cup blueberries
$\frac{1}{2}$ cup black berries
$\frac{1}{2}$ cup chopped carrot
1 cup milk
1 cup cranberry juice
2 cups ice

BRIGHT-EYED STRAWBERRY BANANA BOOST

Strawberries and bananas have always made a tasty combination. And for an added bonus, it's loaded with vitamin C, and protein. A great way to get energized!

1 cup low fat strawberry yogurt
1 cup frozen strawberries
1½ bananas
¾ cup milk

BANANA CRUNCHY

Put away that bowl and spoon and break out the smoothie maker. This smoothie has all the goodness of a breakfast cereal, piece of fruit, and milk rolled into one.

1 cup skim milk
1 banana
2 tbs. honey
½ cup granola
¾ cup ice

BREAKFAST REPLACEMENT SMOOTHIE

This simple all-in-one breakfast smoothie has a nice combination of grain, dairy, fruit, and protein. A great, quick way to jump start your day.

1 banana

2 cups orange juice

½ cup Grape Nut™ breakfast cereal

½ cup, any flavor, low-fat yogurt

1½ cups ice

SMOOTHIE PANCAKES

A new take on pancakes. This maker is quick, easy and has a great nutty taste.

- 1¼ cup water
- 1 cup whole wheat kernels
- ¼ cup non-fat dry milk
- 1 egg
- 2 tbs. oil
- 1 tbs. sugar or honey
- ¼ tsp. salt
- 1 tbs. baking powder

In smoothie maker, mix water, wheat kernels, & dry milk. Blend on smooth for three minutes. Add egg, sugar, and salt. Smooth for 20 seconds. Add baking powder. Pulse three times. Cook immediately on a hot griddle.

MAKE IT A MEAL
LUNCH
SMOOTHIES

HAVING A SMOOTHIE FOR LUNCH can be a great way to boost you energy in the afternoon and keep you going the rest of the day. We've included ingredients that are known to lift spirits and recharge your body. These natural ingredients give you just what you need for a quick and easy lunch without weighing you down or making you sleepy like a big meal might.

PINEAPPLE MANGO PICK-ME-UP

Around noon we often start to feel tired. This can occur because of low blood sugar. Instead of opting to skip lunch to save time or grabbing fast food, why not opt for this protein and fiber filled smoothie.

  1 cup non fat vanilla yogurt
  1 cup pineapple
  ½ cup pineapple juice
  1 cup mango
  1 cup ice
  2 tbs. almond butter

TART TREAT

Sometimes a healthy snack in the middle of the day is better then a full meal. Here is a tart, tasty, smoothie that will refresh and help keep you focused.

  2 cups lemonade
  2 cups frozen strawberries
  1 cup low fat raspberry yogurt
  1 cup ice

ENERGIZING FRUIT SMOOTHIE

This delicious, shippable lunch is packed with nutrients. Use yogurt, orange juice, and a banana as the base and then experiment with a combination of fresh or frozen fruits. This smoothie also adds an extra dose of fiber, a nutrient that a lot of us don't get enough of.

2 cups vanilla nonfat yogurt

2 bananas

2 cups frozen strawberries or peaches

¼ cup orange juice

GO GO JUICE

Fruit is a great pick me up in the middle of the day. This smoothie is a unique blend of fruits that will put some kick into your afternoon and help you get going.

1 cup frozen orange juice concentrate

1 cup pineapple juice

1 cup banana

1 cup passion fruit

½ cup water

1 cup ice

MAKE IT A MEAL
DINNER
SMOOTHIES

SMOOTHIES ARE SO VERSATILE you can even substitute your favorites for an evening meal. If your feeling like eating light, looking for a late evening snack, appetizer or dessert. Smoothies are great for any of these uses. Not only do they taste great, but they provide nutrition in a unique way.

THIRTY SECOND DYNAMITE DINNER

You can add different fruit to this basic smoothie to fit your mood. It's great for a snack before or after dinner, and it's packed with protein.

1 cup peaches
1 cup milk
2 tbs. Wheat germ
dash nutmeg
dash cinnamon
1½ cups ice

SHRIMP COCKTAIL

This smoothie is filling enough to be a meal. The great blend of veggies and shrimp provide plenty of protein, vitamins, and fiber. Or use it as an appetizer when entertaining. Your guests will love it!

46 oz. tomato juice
1 cup ketchup
1 tbs. horse radish
1 tsp. garlic powder
1 pinch salt
1 tsp. sugar
1 tbs. lemon juice
1 cup chopped celery
1 cup chopped carrot
2 cans small shrimp
½ cup ice (optional)

PEANUT BUTTER BANANA SMOOTHIE

This sweet treat is packed with protein, carbohydrates, and potassium. You'll get a quick pick-up to carry you through to the next meal.

1/2 cup peanut butter

1 cup milk

1/2 cup vanilla ice cream

2 bananas

1/4 tsp. vanilla

2 cups ice

AWESOME ORANGE AVOCADO

This different recipe will impress you and your guests. The avocado gives this smoothie a great texture. No one will ever guess what's giving your smoothie its beautiful green color.

2 cups orange juice

1 1/2 cups pineapple or orange sherbet

1 cup strawberries (fresh or frozen)

2 bananas

2 tbs. honey

1 avocado peeled and sliced

1 1/2 cups ice

SMOOTHIES FOR

SPECIAL OCCASIONS

SMOOTHIES AND ENTERTAINING go hand in hand. They help turn any dinner party into a special occasion. Great for summer parties, Christmas get togethers, or any time you are looking to spice up your gathering.

TROPICAL PARADISE

This smoothie brings the tropics right to your living room or back yard. Not only is it delicious, but it's good for you too!

    2 cups pineapple-orange juice
    1 banana
    1 can (8 oz) pineapple chunks with juice
    2 cups frozen vanilla yogurt
    2 tbs. flaked coconut
    1½ cups ice

OCEAN SURPRISE

    2 cups raspberry juice
    2 cups orange sherbet
    1 cup strawberries
    1 banana
    1½ cups ice

PUMPKIN SMOOTHIE

This is a great smoothie any time. Try adding it to your thanksgiving feast. It makes a fabulous pre-dinner drink or side-kick for your thanksgiving leftovers. Pumpkin is a hearty vegetable that gives this smoothie great texture and is packed with vitamins and iron.

    1 cup canned pumpkin
    1 cup apricot (canned or fresh)
    2 tbs. sugar
    1 cup milk
    dash cinnamon
    dash nutmeg
    1½ cups ice

EGGNOG SMOOTHIE

A great take on an old favorite. This frozen concoction is great any time of year. Serve it a Christmas parties, it will quickly become a new favorite.

    2 cups eggnog
    1 banana
    1 cup nonfat vanilla yogurt
    ½ cup milk
    2 cups ice
    dash nutmeg

MARGARITA

1 cup margarita mix (sweet & sour mix)
2 tbs. lime juice
1½ cups ice
*dip rim of glass in water, then salt. Garnish with a lime

PIÑA COLADA

2 cups pineapple juice
½ cup cream of coconut, or coconut milk
1 cup plain nonfat yogurt
1 cup ice
*top with whipped cream

PEACH DAIQUIRI

With this recipe, you can replace the peaches with your favorite fruit for a refreshing smoothie any season!

1 cup frozen peaches

1 cup lemon lime soda

2 tbs. half & half

2 tbs. sugar

1 cup ice

GERMAN CHOCOLATE SMOOTHIE

This rich smoothie is yummy as a dessert at parties or any-time. It's a light alternative to the favorite pastry.

2 cups chocolate ice cream

1 cup coconut milk

1 tbs. flaked coconut

¼ cup chopped pecans

1 tbs. caramel ice cream topping

¾ cup ice

FRUITY FRAPPE

This frothy smoothie is a delightful blend of fruit, that is perfect for a brunch, or special luncheon, but easy enough to make any time you're looking for a light, great-tasting snack.

  2 cups pineapple sherbet
  ½ cup frozen raspberries
  ¼ cup frozen blueberries
  ¼ cup frozen boysenberries
  1 banana
  1½ cups lemon lime soda
  ½ cup ice

KEY LIME SMOOTHIE

A new twist on an old favorite. This smoothie is rich and surprisingly refreshing. It's easy enough to whip up when company drops in and is sure to have the raving.

  1 can (14 oz.) sweetened condensed milk
  1 cup plain yogurt
  1 banana
  ⅓ cup key lime juice (fresh or concentrate)
  1 cup ice

FROZEN RASPBERRY LEMONADE

Now you can make this drug store favorite at home!

2 cups lemonade

1 cup raspberries (fresh or frozen)

2 cups raspberry sherbet

1 cup ice

CHOCOLATE-PEANUT BUTTER BLAST

1 cup milk

2 cups vanilla frozen yogurt

2 tsp. malt

¼ cup peanut butter

1 tbs. chocolate syrup

1-1½ cups ice

FROSTY FRUIT SMOOTHIE

1 banana
1 cup grape juice
½ cup pineapple chunks
½ of an orange, peeled
½ cup milk
1 tbs. sugar
1 tsp. vanilla
1 cup ice

BLACKBERRY CREAM-SICLE

Lime juice gives this sweet smoothie just a taste of tart.
2 cups vanilla ice cream
1 cup frozen blackberries
½ cup frozen strawberries
1½ cups milk
½ tsp. lime juice
*garnish with blackberries and whipped cream

ORANGE ALMOND WHIP

This smoothie combines several favorite tastes and whips them up. It's a recipe you'll come back to again and again.

3 oz. frozen orange juice concentrate

3 oz. frozen lemonade concentrate

2 tbs. sugar

½ tsp. almond extract

2 cups water

1 -1½ cups ice

STRAWBERRY CHEESECAKE SMOOTHIE

You can never go wrong with cheesecake. Now you can have it anytime with only half the guilt. This smoothie version of the classic desert is lower in calories and fat, but high in taste!

3 oz. cream cheese softened

1 can sweetened condensed milk

1 banana

1 cup strawberries (fresh or frozen)

1 can (8 oz.) crushed pineapple, with juice

2 tbs. lemon juice concentrate

1 cup ice

*garnish with strawberries if desired

SHAVED
ICE

FAVORITES

THE HOME ICE SHAVER has brought with it scores of shaved ice treat ideas. We have moved way beyond simple snow cones. Don't misunderstand – snow cones are still a quick, easy treat on a hot summer day. However, you can do so much more with shaved ice, that we just had to throw in a few of our favorite ice treat recipes.

SLUSH VARIATIONS

SOFT DRINK SLUSH
Fill a glass with shaved ice and add your favorite soda such as Cherry 7-Up, Slice, Pepsi, Coca Cola, regular or diet. Cool, simple and so sooooothing!

FRUIT JUICE SLUSHES
Add fruit juice such as apple, grape, orange, grapefruit, or other favorite to shaved ice. A natural refresher.

LEMONADE SLUSH
Shaved ice is a perfect addition to lemonades. Try pink lemonade and shaved ice for a fun party drink.

FRUIT FREEZE
Place 2 cups shaved ice into your blender. Add ½ cup fruit and ½ cup fruit juice. Process until ultra smooth. For a thicker slush add more shaved ice.

TROPICAL BREEZE
Combine equal amounts of pineapple, apple, and orange juices. Pour over a tall glass of shaved ice and garnish with fruit slice or maraschino cherry. Aloha!

SUN-RISE DELIGHT

½ cold cantaloupe

1 cup watermelon balls or honeydew balls

½ cup grapes (optional)

¼ cup apple juice, orange or pineapple

2 cups shaved ice

Make melon balls from ½ cantaloupe and scoop out rind completely to make a bowl. Fill cantaloupe bowl with ice and fruit. Sprinkle with juice. A real eye-opener!

FROSTED FRUIT

½ cup blueberries

1 peach, pitted & sliced

6 cherries, unstemmed

1 tsp. sugar

1 lime, juiced

2 cups shaved ice

Place in a chilled breakfast bowl. Add fruit mix gently. Sprinkle with lime juice and sugar.

FRUIT & ORANGE CREAM

    1 peach, pitted and thin sliced

    ½ banana, sliced

    ⅓ cup cream or milk

    1 tsp. sugar

    1 cherry, unstemmed for garnish (optional)

    1 cup orange juice, frozen

Freeze orange juice in ice cube mold. Shave into chilled breakfast bowl. Add peach and banana slices, then pour on cream. Sprinkle on sugar and garnish with a single cherry. You'll wake up with a smile!

RASPBERRY SORBET

    2 cups fresh raspberries (or blackberries)

    ¼ cup sugar

    ½ cup water

    1 tbs. lemon juice

    1 tbs. orange juice

    2 cups shaved ice

Combine raspberries and water in a food processor or blender and puree until smooth. Strain through a fine sieve into mixing bowl. Add remaining ingredients and stir until sugar is dissolved. Pour over shaved ice and enjoy.

RASPBERRY VELVET

1 cup raspberries (fresh or frozen)

2 tbs. raspberry preserves

$\frac{1}{2}$ cup heavy cream

3 cups cranberry juice

4 cups shaved

Combine all ingredients except ice in a blender and process until smooth. Continue to blend while adding shaved ice until the mixture has a sherbet-like consistency. Pour into stemmed glasses and garnish with a big red raspberry. Perfect! Serve immediately.

PEACH REFRESHER

2 fresh peaches, pared and quartered

   or

1 can (16 oz) can peaches, drained

2 cups lemon-lime carbonated beverage

$\frac{1}{2}$ cup cream of coconut cold

$\frac{1}{4}$ cup milk

$1\frac{1}{4}$ cup milk, frozen

3 tbs. maraschino cherry syrup

Combine peaches, cream of coconut, milk and cherry juice in a blender and process until smooth. Shave $1\frac{1}{4}$ cup frozen milk block and add to blender mixture. Process until smooth. Pour equal amounts of mixture into 4 tall glasses. Slowly pour $\frac{1}{2}$ cup lemon-lime soda into each glass. Garnish as desired. Serve immediately.

GRAPE ESCAPE

$\frac{1}{2}$ cup Concord grape juice

$\frac{1}{2}$ cup frozen grape juice concentrate

$\frac{1}{2}$ cup pineapple chunks

1 tbs. lime juice, ginger ale, or 7-Up

2-4 cups shaved ice

Grape clusters for garnish

Blend ingredients except the ginger ale and shaved ice until smooth. Pour into stemmed glass over shaved ice. Top with ginger ale. Stir and garnish with grape clusters.

APPLE-CINNAMON SORBET

    4 golden delicious apples

    ⅓ cup sugar (to taste)

    ½ cup apple juice

    1½ tsp. lemon juice

    ¼ tsp. cinnamon

    2 cups shaved ice

Thin apple slices dipped in lemon juice for garnish

Core, pare and shred apples. Puree all ingredients except shaved ice until smooth. Add shaved ice to blender and continue processing until desired consistency is achieved. Garnish with apple slices.

SMOOTHIES & ICE TREATS

INDEX

Alphabetical

Lindsay Barnes is a nutritionist and smoothie lover from Sandy, Utah.

Amy Shawgo is a writer and full-time mother of five from West Jordan, Utah.